Anansi Stories

Adapted by Sheila Lane and Marion Kemp

Illustrations by David Anstey

Take Part Starters
Level 3

Ward Lock Educational Co. Ltd.

Ward Lock Educational Co. Ltd.
BIC Ling Kee House
1 Christopher Road
East Grinstead
Sussex RH19 3BT

A member of the Ling Kee Group
London · Hong Kong · New York · Singapore

This adaptation published 1989
© Sheila Lane and Marion Kemp
ISBN 0 7062 5081 8

Reprinted 1996, 1998

Printed in Hong Kong

Contents

★ This sign means that you can make
the sounds which go with the story.

Anansi and the Bananas

In this story you will read about:

Anansi, the Spider Man,

Anansi's Wife,

Carly, Anansi's daughter,

and Sam, Anansi's son

Anansi comes into the kitchen carrying three big bananas. ★

Anansi Hallo, children!
Look what your clever Daddy has brought home.

Wife Listen to him, children!

Anansi Your clever Daddy has been to the market and bought the three biggest bananas in the whole world.

Wife Just listen to that man!

Anansi What's troubling you, woman?

Wife You're troubling me, Anansi.

Anansi How's that?

Wife Carly! Count the folks who live in this house.

Carly Daddy . . . one! Sam . . . two! You . . . three!
And me . . . four!

Wife Just so! Now, Sam, count those bananas.

Sam One . . . two . . . three! Three bananas.

Wife Just so! Your Daddy has bought THREE bananas
for FOUR people. You're a gump, Anansi!
You're a great big gump!

Anansi Listen to me, woman! There's no problem with
these bananas. Here, Carly-girl! You take this one.

Carly Thank you, Daddy-man.

Anansi Here, Sam! You take this one.

Sam Thank you, Daddy-man.

Wife What about me?

Anansi Here you are, woman.
You take this last one.

6

Carly But that's ALL the bananas, Daddy.

Sam And you like bananas too, Daddy-man.

Wife You like eating next best to sleeping, Anansi.

Anansi Well, I guess I'll
just have sleeping today.
I'll lay myself
down here while
my family eat their
bananas.

Hush up now, everybody!
Anansi is going to
get a bit of shut-eye
while you all eat
your bananas!

Wife Well! Well! Well!
Your Daddy is acting
very strange, today,
children!

Sam   Look at him!

Carly   He's asleep already. ★
Listen to him snoring!

Wife   Carly! Go and check on him.
That Daddy of yours
is full of tricks.

Carly   Daddy IS sleeping. ★
Listen to him!

Wife   Do as I say, Carly!
Check on him.

Carly   I know what I'll do!
I'll pull his hair.

Anansi   OW! OW!
What's that?
Hush up and let
me get a bit
of shut-eye!

Wife Sam! You go and check on him this time.
Like I said, that Daddy of yours is
full of tricks.

Sam Listen! ★
He's sleeping.

Wife Do as I say, Sam.
Check on him.

Sam I know what I'll do!
I'll pull his leg.

Anansi OW! OW!
Can't you let a man sleep?

Wife We're just checking on you
before we eat our bananas.

Anansi Bananas! Ah, bananas!
Beautiful bananas!
How I do love eating
bananas.

Carly   Please, Daddy!
Take half of my banana.

Anansi   No, no, Carly-girl.
Your Daddy couldn't do that.

Carly   Please! PLEASE, Daddy!
Take half.

Anansi   OK! OK! Just to
please you, little one . . .
Just one little half!
But no more, please!

Sam   Please, Daddy!
Take half of this one.

Anansi   No, Sammy!
Your Daddy couldn't do that.

Sam   Please! PLEASE, Daddy!
Take half.

Anansi   OK! OK! I'll take half . . .
But no more, please!

Carly I've given half of my banana to Daddy.

Sam And I've given half of my banana to Daddy.

Carly Mammy! YOU give half of YOUR banana to Daddy.

Sam Yes, Mammy! You do that!

Anansi No, no, children! I couldn't take half of
your Mammy's banana.

Wife Listen to him!

Carly Mammy! Ask Daddy to take half of your banana.

Sam Yes, Mammy! You do that.

Wife Will you take half of my banana, Anansi?

Anansi No, no, woman! Nothing in the world would
make me take half of your banana.

Wife Listen to him!

Sam   Mammy! Make him take half of your banana.

Wife   Go on, Anansi! Take it!

Sam   Go on, Daddy! Take it!

Anansi   I've told you – NO!

Wife   You'd better take it, Anansi.
If you don't, I'll . . .

Anansi   What? What will you do?

Wife   I'll leave you! That's it!
If you don't take half
of my banana . . .
I'LL LEAVE YOU!

Sam   No, Mammy! ★

Carly   Don't do that, Mammy! ★

Wife   Now look what you've done, Anansi!
The children are crying their eyes out. ★

Anansi Stop crying, children!
I'll take half of your Mammy's banana.

Wife Just look at your Daddy's
plate now, children!

Carly He's got my half
banana . . .

Sam . . . and my half banana . . .

Wife . . . and MY half banana.

Carly That makes ONE AND A
HALF bananas on
Daddy's plate.

Wife I guess your Daddy isn't such a gump
after all, children!
But just you wait, Anansi!
Just you wait!

Anansi and the Hot Hatful

In this story you will read about:

Anansi,

Anansi's Wife,

Carly,

and Sam.

Anansi comes into the kitchen wearing his big garden hat. ★

Anansi My wife said,
'Be sure you give that
stew a good stir while
we're at the market, Anansi.
Make sure that the rice
doesn't stick to the pot'.

So that's what I'm doing.

'Stir it, Anansi,' she said,
'STIR IT, but DON'T EAT IT.'

Mmm! ★ It smells good. ★
Maybe I should try it! ★

YUM! ★ It tastes good!

Maybe I should try
a bit more . . . ★

YUM! ★ It tastes . . .

SAKES ALIVE! ★
Who's that coming? ★

Sam Daddy! Daddy!

Carly   Hallo, Daddy! We're back from the market.

Anansi   Where's your Mammy?

Carly   She's coming along the road with the potatoes.

Anansi   Then you get back along that road and help
your Mammy to carry those potatoes.
Go on! Both of you! Hurry up! BIRD SPEED! ★

Anansi   Now!
How can I get myself a
big helping of this stew
before my wife comes back?

I know!
I'll put a big helping
onto this dish . . .
NO! If I do that,
she'll know!

★ OH! They're coming!

I know!
I'll put it into my hat! ★

Wife   Anansi! Anansi! Where IS that man?

Sam   He's not here, Mammy!

Wife   Not here! Then I guess
that Daddy of yours has let
the stew stick to the pot.

Sam   Come and see, Mammy.

Carly   It smells good! ★ YUM!

Wife   Just look in this pot, children!
Our stew is half gone!

Carly   It's half gone, Sam! Look!

Sam   Look at that!

Wife   I guess somebody has been in this kitchen and
helped himself to our stew! And I guess I
know who that somebody is!
Find that Daddy of yours, children!

Sam   Come on, Carly! Let's go! ★

Anansi   She's coming!
She'll skin me alive for this.
What shall I do?
Where can I hide this stew?

I know!
I'll put my hat
back on my head . . .!
Here goes . . .!
OUCH!

Sam   Daddy! Daddy!
Where are you?

Carly   There he is!
He's hiding behind the Cassava bush!

Anansi Howdy, folks! OUCH!

Sam Look at him, Mammy!

Carly What's troubling you, Daddy?

Anansi OUCH! OUCH! ★

Carly He's jumping about like a cat on a hot tin roof!

Anansi OUCH! OUCH! ★
It's all in my head!

Wife It's not! That stew of ours is all in your inside.

Anansi What ARE you talking about, woman?

Wife Our stew! I'm talking about our stew. 'STIR IT', I said . . . 'DON'T EAT IT!'

Anansi I did stir it . . . and then . . .

Wife And then you ATE it!

Sam   Look at him!

Carly   What's biting you, Daddy?

Anansi   Did you say, 'What's biting you?'

Wife   That's what she said!

Anansi   That's it! There's a big bee biting me!

Sam   Where, Daddy? Where is it biting you?

Anansi   Under my hat!

Wife   So that's where it is! Let's have
your hat off your head, Anansi!

Anansi   NO! NO! Leave my hat . . .

Wife   I'm going to get that hat
off your head!

Anansi   Don't touch my hat, woman!

Wife   I'm going to take that hat
right off your head!

20

Carly   That's it! Let the poor bee
out of your hat, Daddy.

Sam   So it can fly away.

Anansi   Leave it, children!
Don't touch my hat.

Wife   Hold on to your Daddy's
legs, children.

Carly   I'll hold these two!

Sam   And I'll hold these two!

Anansi   NO! NO! NO!
Let me go!

Wife   I'm going to take that
hat off your head, Anansi,
if it's the last thing I do!

Anansi   OH! OH! OH!
Leave me, I say!
Leave me!

21

Family   WOW!

Sam   Look at him!

Wife   Just so!
Your Daddy had . . .
rice . . . and peas
. . . and peppers
. . . and beans
under his hat!

Carly   But no bee!

Wife   Just so!
No bee and no brains!

Carly   And no hair!

Sam   Look at his head!

Carly   He's lost all his hair!

Anansi   OW! OW! I'm bald!

Wife   You're bald as
a coot, Anansi!

Family Ha! Ha! Ha! Ha!

Anansi What shall I do? Everyone will laugh
when they see my bald head.

Carly You will have to hide yourself away, Daddy.

Anansi What shall I do? Where shall I go?

Sam You will have to stay in the house, Daddy-man.

Wife Just so, Anansi! You will have to stay
indoors till your hair grows again.

Anansi Oh! Oh! What shall I do?

Wife You can stay in the house and do the work.

Anansi ME! But . . .

Wife No BUTS!
You can stay indoors
and do the work and
I'll go out and enjoy myself!

Anansi and the Magic Cook-Pot

In this story you will read about:

Anansi,

Carly,

Sam,

and the Magic Cook-Pot.

Anansi comes into the kitchen carrying buckets, brooms, mops and dusters. ★

Anansi Sakes alive!
Just look at me!
My wife said,
'You stay indoors
and do the work,
Anansi, while I
go out and enjoy
myself!'
That woman!

Fancy a big man
like me . . .
sweeping . . .
washing . . .
dusting . . . ★

Who's that calling?

Sam ME!

Anansi SAKES ALIVE!
That's Sam calling
from the yard.

Sam   DADDY! DADDY!

Anansi   That boy! STAY OUT THERE, SAM!

Sam   But Daddy!

Anansi   Stay out there
in the yard, Sam.
Your Daddy is
cleaning the house. ★

Sam   DADDY! ★ DADDY!

Anansi   Sakes alive! What will I do to that boy?
WHAT'S THE MATTER WITH YOU?

Sam   I want a drink of water.

Anansi   Water lives in the tap, Sam-boy. You go
and get it for yourself from the tap in the yard.

Sam   No! No! I can't do that.
Mammy says . . .

Anansi   Your Mammy's not here, boy. She's out enjoying herself.
Fancy that! She's OUT and I'm IN here doing the work!

Carly DADDY! DADDY! ★

Anansi That girl!
STAY OUT THERE, CARLY!

Carly But Daddy!

Anansi Don't YOU start
wanting something, Carly.
Your Daddy is cleaning the house.

Carly DADDY! ★ I'M HUNGRY!

Anansi You must wait till dinner-time, Carly-girl.

Carly Can I have a cookie?

Anansi No cookies till dinner-time! That's what
your Mammy says.

Carly Mammy gives me a bit of fruit when I'm hungry. She gives
me a bit of melon . . . or . . . an apple. Can I have an apple?

Anansi Well . . . just one little apple.

Carly I'll come in and get it. ★

Sam   DADDY! DADDY! Is Carly in there?

Anansi   Sakes alive! Now that boy will want to come in!

Sam   I want an apple. Carly has got an apple . . .!

Anansi   OK! OK! Come in and get yourself an apple, Sam.
You come in and I'll go out!

Carly   You can't go out, Daddy. If you go out
everybody will see your bald head.

Anansi   Sam! Where's that woolly hat
you wear in the cold weather?

Sam   Here it is, Daddy-man.

Anansi   I'll put Sam's hat
on my head . . . so!
Now . . . out I go!

Carly   But it's nearly
dinner-time, Daddy!

Sam   DINNER! I want my dinner!

Anansi   I'm locking these children in and I'm going OUT! ★

Anansi   Those children! They tire a man out!
I'll rest up under this bread-fruit tree
and get myself a bit of shut-eye.
Sweet dreams, Anansi-man! Sweet dreams! ★

Anansi   Sakes alive! Who are you?

Pot   What do I look like?

Anansi   You look like a cooking pot.

Pot   I AM a cooking pot.

Anansi   Is that so? Well, I wish you were full
of good, hot dinner.

Pot   Say, 'COOK – POT – COOK!' and I will be.

Anansi   Sakes alive! OK, then! I will.
COOK – POT – COOK!

Pot   Help yourself! ★

Anansi Listen, Cook-Pot! I've got an idea. Will you come and live in my fine house and help me to feed my family?

Pot Well . . . maybe . . . I shall have to think about it.

Anansi I'll take good care of you. I'll give you a good home and keep you clean . . .

Pot NO! NO! You mustn't do that. You must NEVER clean me.

Anansi Never clean you?

Pot Never! Never! NEVER!

Anansi Why is that?

Pot If you wash me out I can never cook again.

Anansi OK! OK! I'll take you home and I'LL NEVER wash you out. Come on, Cook-Pot! My children are waiting for their dinner.

Anansi Hallo, children! Look what I've got.

Carly I don't want a cooking pot!

Sam I want my DINNER!

Anansi What do you want for
dinner today, children?

Carly A big beef and
rice stew with beans . . .

Sam . . . and peas . . .

Carly . . . and peppers!

Anansi OK! OK! Now watch your Daddy
make a big beef and rice stew.
Listen to this . . . COOK – POT – COOK!

Pot Help yourself!

Sam Look at that!

Carly It's a MAGIC cooking pot!

Pot Come on! Help yourself. ★

32

Anansi Now, Cook-Pot!
I'll hide you up here
where no-one
can find you.

Pot OK! OK!
That's fine.

Anansi You will be
quite safe here
while I'm away.

Pot Away! Where are
you going?

Anansi I'm just going out
for a walk after
that good dinner.

Pot OK! OK!
But don't be long! ★

Carly Look out of the window, Sam, and tell me
when Daddy has gone down the road.

Sam ★ He's gone!

Carly OK. Now I'll tell you what we'll do.
We'll get the Magic Cook-Pot down
and make another dinner for ourselves.

Sam Ooo! Ooo! I'll get it.

Carly No you won't, Sam. It was MY idea, so I'll get it.
You can get the chair. Go on! Get the chair!

Sam OK! ★ Here it is! ★

Carly Now . . . you hold the chair and I'll
climb up and get the Pot down. ★

Pot Hallo, children! What do you want?

Sam We want some dinner.

Pot But you've just had your dinner.

Sam Yes! But we want some more.

Pot If you want some more dinner,
you must say the Magic Words.

Carly I know what to say.

Sam So do I!

Sam & Carly COOK – POT – COOK!

Pot Help yourself! ★

Sam Yum! Yum! ★ This is good!

Carly Thank you, Cook-Pot. This is
the best dinner I've ever had.

Sam I want some more.

Pot Help yourself! ★

Carly I'll have some more too . . .   more . . . and more . . .
and more . . .

35

Carly Sam! Listen! ★ I think I can hear someone coming.

Sam I'll look out of the window. ★

Carly Who is it?

Sam It's Daddy! He's coming along the road.

Carly We must put the Cook-Pot back on the shelf before he comes in.

Sam OK, Carly! I'll do it.

Carly Not yet, Sam! We must clean it first!

Pot CLEAN me!

Carly Yes! Clean you!

Pot Not ME!

Sam Yes! . . . YOU!

Pot No! No! NO! You must NEVER clean me.

Carly Mammy ALWAYS cleans her cooking pots. Come on, Sam! Help me to wash this Cook-Pot!

Pot   Don't do it, I say! DON'T DO IT!

Carly   Don't listen, Sam. Help me to
rub it really clean, like this. ★

Sam   But Daddy-man will be here!

Carly   Not yet! Rub harder, Sam! ★ Rub harder! ★

Pot   You'll be sorry for this . . . SORRY, I TELL YOU!

Carly   Oh no we won't! We've made you really clean
so Daddy won't know that we've had another dinner.

Sam   He's coming! ★ He's coming!

Anansi What are you doing to my Magic Cook-Pot children?

Carly Nothing, Daddy-man!

Sam Nothing at all!

Anansi Have you been playing with my Cook-Pot?

Carly Oh, no Daddy. We haven't been PLAYING with it.

Anansi Sam! Come here! ★
What were you doing with my Cook-Pot?

Sam We were helping you, Daddy-man.

Anansi HELPING! Sakes alive! You don't sound like
my children at all! Now! What were you doing?

Carly We were cleaning the Cook-Pot for you, Daddy.

Anansi SAKES ALIVE! Not CLEANING it!

Sam Yes! We were cleaning it.

Carly We were cleaning it like Mammy cleans her
cooking pots.

Anansi   You bad children! I'll skin you both alive for this!

Carly   But Mammy ALWAYS cleans her cooking pot before she puts it back in the cupboard.

Anansi   This isn't your Mammy's pot. This is MY pot . . . and now it isn't MAGIC any more.

Sam   Not magic?

Carly   Why?

Anansi   You've washed all the magic away, that's why!

Carly   What shall we do?

Sam   Oh! Oh! ★ What shall we do?

Anansi   You'll go hungry! That's what you'll do!

Ask your teacher to read you some more Anansi Stories.

This is Sam
saying one
of his parts:

I know what I'll do!
I'll pull his leg.

Who said each of these parts?

That Daddy of yours
is full of tricks.

No! No! NO!
You must
NEVER
clean me.

He's jumping about
like a cat on a hot
tin roof!

Hush up and let me
get a bit of shut-eye!